Space Exploration

KINGFISHER
LONDON & NEW YORK

KINGFISHER
LONDON & NEW YORK

Text and design copyright © Toucan Books Ltd. 2013, 2019
Based on an original idea by Toucan Books Ltd.
Illustrations copyright © Simon Basher 2013, 2019

First published in 2013
This edition published in the United States by Kingfisher in 2019,
175 Fifth Ave., New York, NY 10010
Kingfisher is an imprint of Macmillan Children's Books, London.

Consultants: Carole Stott and Giles Sparrow

Designed and created by Basher www.basherbooks.com
Text written by Dan Green

Dedicated to Otto Wilkinson

Distributed in the U.S. and Canada by Macmillan, 175 Fifth Ave., New York, NY 10010

Library of Congress Cataloging-in-Publication Data has been applied for.

ISBN 978-0-7534-7506-5

Kingfisher books are available for special promotions and premiums.
For details contact: Special Markets Department, Macmillan,
175 Fifth Avenue, New York, NY 10010.

For more information, please visit: www.kingfisherbooks.com

Printed in China
9 8 7 6 5 4 3 2 1
1TR/0319/WKT/UG/128MA

CONTENTS

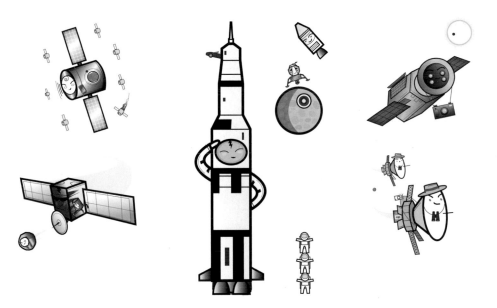

Introduction
The Moon Landing

Alarms sound in the cramped spaceship as it speeds across the surface of the Moon. Some 238,855 miles (384,400km) from home, the autopilot computer overloads. Neil Armstrong takes the controls and flies solo. He skims over a jumble of rocks and boulders and plows on, ice-cool, looking for a safe place to set down the delicate spacecraft. With just 30 seconds of fuel remaining, he touches down on the surface of the Moon. The Eagle has landed!

Six and a half hours later, Neil Armstrong and "Buzz" Aldrin exit the Apollo 11 lunar lander. Armstrong swings out onto the rickety ladder, before jumping into the unknown, becoming the first person to step foot on another world. He says the famous words, "That's one small step for [a] man, one giant leap for mankind." Unlike other types of exploration, which claim new territories and riches for nations, space exploration is for all of humankind. The idea is that outside the boundaries of our planet our differences become unimportant in the vastness of space.

"We come in peace for all mankind."

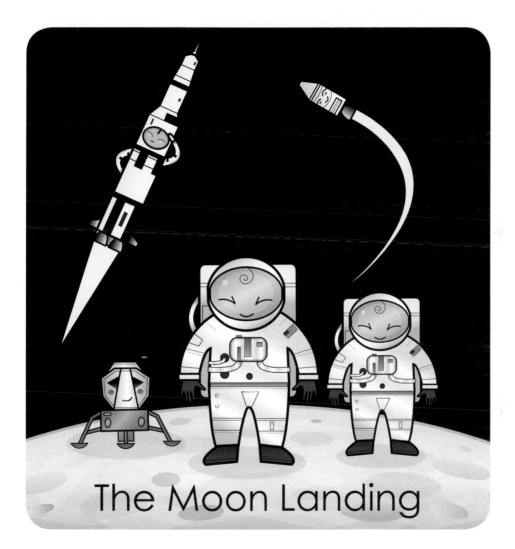

The Moon Landing

Chapter 1
Space Aces

Meet the Space Aces, a high-flying bunch of dreamers. The people taking to the air with this set of sky-skimmers have traveled faster than humans have ever gone before. They have also ridden their luck and taken risks that would scare your mother silly! The first humans to go into space were test pilots—they were the only ones crazy enough to sit on top of a missile and say, "Light it!" And yet, Houston, we clearly have a problem! Yes, the Space Aces may "rock"-et, but really they have only just scratched the surface of the Great Unknown: most space flights barely even clear Earth's atmosphere.

Sputnik 1

Orbit

Space Shuttle

Rocket

Space Suit

International
Space Station

Falcon

Sputnik 1
■ Space Aces

✷ Earth's very first artificial satellite
✷ Transmitted its bleep for 22 days until its batteries ran down
✷ Kick-started the Space Race between the Soviets and the U.S.A.

Back in the day, it was me who showed the world that human-made objects could be placed in orbit around Earth and above the atmosphere. No bigger than an exercise ball with four long, trailing antennae, I looked like a metal jellyfish. Once above Earth, I started to transmit my beep-beep message and my signal was picked up all around the world by radio hacks.

Sputnik 1

● Launch date: October 4, 1957
● Size of metal sphere: 23 in. (58.5cm) in diameter
● Number of Earth orbits: 1,440

✴ The curved path an object makes around a planet, moon, or star
✴ Objects can be human-made (e.g. probe) or natural (e.g. Earth)
✴ An object in orbit around Earth is called a satellite

Orbit

I am a whirling dervish! I'm the path around, say, a planet, that an object follows when its forward motion balances out the planet's pull of gravity. This is how the Moon circles Earth and Earth circles the Sun. If an object traveled any faster, it would shoot off into space; any slower and it would crash down to the ground. With me about, the object stays firmly on its curved course.

● First object to orbit Earth: 1957 (Sputnik 1, U.S.S.R.)
● First human to orbit Earth: 1961 (Yuri Gagarin, U.S.S.R.)
● Official start of space: 60 mi. (100km) (known as the Kármán line)

Space Shuttle
■ Space Aces

✳ The first reusable, winged "space plane"
✳ The five shuttles included Discovery, Endeavour, and Atlantis
✳ Challenger and Columbia were lost in fatal accidents

I'm the Granddaddy—the largest spacecraft ever to travel to space. I'm retired now, but for a good 30 years I was the workhorse of the U.S. space program. I lifted and carried people and equipment into low Earth orbit (LEO).

I had space for two satellites or a space lab in my payload bay. I took the Hubble Space Telescope into orbit and transported many International Space Station modules. Made from clip-together parts, I had a space plane called the Orbiter with a big, external fuel tank (ET) slung beneath and two solid rocket boosters (SRBs) clipped to that. Firing both SRBs and the main engines, I took to the skies. After two minutes, the burned-out SRBs were jettisoned; six minutes later, the ET was released. Gliding back to Earth, my Orbiter would touch down at 220 mph (350km/h). Happy days!

● First Space Shuttle flight: April 12, 1981 (Columbia)
● Last Space Shuttle lands after final flight: July 21, 2011 (Atlantis)
● Number of Space Shuttle launches: 135

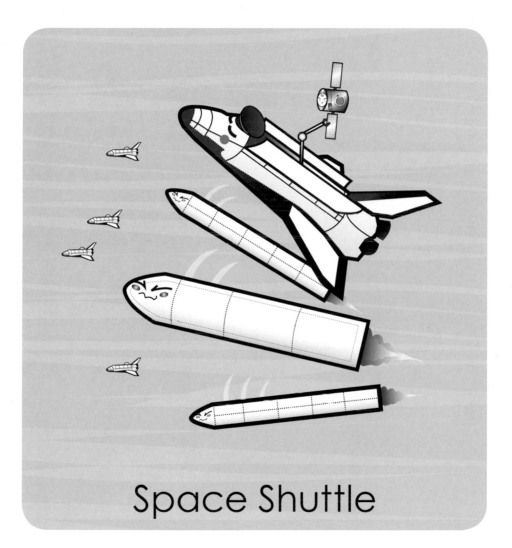

Space Shuttle

Rocket
■ Space Aces

✳ Gravity-beating engine that lifts things into space
✳ Works by throwing exhaust gases out behind it at high speed
✳ The speed needed to beat gravity is called "escape velocity"

5...4...3...2...1—life's a blast with me around! I'm used for carrying stuff to space. I am a reaction engine, which means I create forward thrust by throwing mass at high speeds out of my rear end. Rocket scientists design me with multiple "stages," which are ditched when used up to reduce my weight in flight. Some of my newest models use less fuel so don't have stages.

Rocket

● Escape velocity (Earth): 7 mi. (11km) per second (24,850 mi./40,000km per hour)
● First rocket to reach space: 1957 (R-7, U.S.S.R.)
● Fuel consumption of Saturn V's "F1" engines: 5.2 in. to the gal. (3.5cm to the L)

Space Suit

Space Aces ■

✳ Tough protection for astronauts outside their spacecraft
✳ Features a bubble helmet with a gold, radiation-blocking visor
✳ Color-coded legs help identify astronauts in space

Space Suit

Hi! I'm an Extravehicular Mobility Unit (EMU for short). My pressurized suit stops blood and body fluids boiling in space. As many as 14 layers offer comfort and safety. The outer shell is made from supertough Kevlar, which provides protection from micrometeorites. My life-support system provides oxygen to breathe, and my gloves have a heater in each finger.

● Number of parts in a typical space suit: about 18,000
● Length of pipes in undergarments: 300 ft. (91.5m)
● Typical weight: 276 lb. (125kg)

International Space Station

✳ AKA the ISS—an orbiting space laboratory in low Earth orbit
✳ Built from 1998 to 2011, using contributions from 16 nations
✳ The third-brightest object in the sky after the Sun and Moon

Cruisin' at 240 mi. (390km) above Earth, I'm like a diamond in the sky. The most expensive science project *ever*, I'm a bustling space hub, built piece by piece over more than ten years.

I'm built on a long truss bolted together in space. Off this structure hang double-sided, Sun-tracking solar arrays that provide power, temperature-regulating radiators, living quarters, and laboratories. Life is buzzing with plenty of experiments to fill a ten-hour working day. Astronauts stay for up to six months, breathing stale air and drinking (ahem) "recycled" water, eating ready-made dinners, and sleeping tethered to a metal wall. However, they do get to see 15 sunrises and sunsets *every* day. Beat that, Earth dwellers!

● First component launched: 1998 (Zarya, Russian Federal Space Agency)
● Orbital speed: 17,210 mph (27,700km/h)
● Living space: 13,702 cu. ft. (388 cu. m)

International
Space Station

Falcon
■ Space Aces

✹ Multi-use space-launch vehicles made by SpaceX
✹ Named after the *Millennium Falcon* in the *Star Wars* film series
✹ Falcon Heavy is the fourth-most powerful space rocket

Meet the Falcon team—a happy family of space truckers. We're in the business of haulage and heavy lifting. Our rockets transport astronauts and supplies into space. Like all rockets, we blast off vertically, but what sets us apart is that we are designed to land when we come back to Earth. Yup, we are reusable!

Falcon 9 does regular deliveries to the ISS, while our newest family member, Falcon Heavy, could one day take robot space probes to Mars. As it thunders off the launchpad, Falcon Heavy gives out the same thrust as 18 jumbo jets. In 2018, it sent a Tesla Roadster sports car spinning toward the Red Planet, top down and blaring out David Bowie's "Life on Mars." From the 2020s, BFR (Big Falcon Rocket) will take crewed launches to the Moon and Mars.

● Height (Falcon Heavy): 229.6 ft. (70m)
● Mass (Falcon Heavy): 3,125,735 lb. (1,420,788kg)
● Super heavy-lift class: lifts more than 50 tons in low Earth orbit

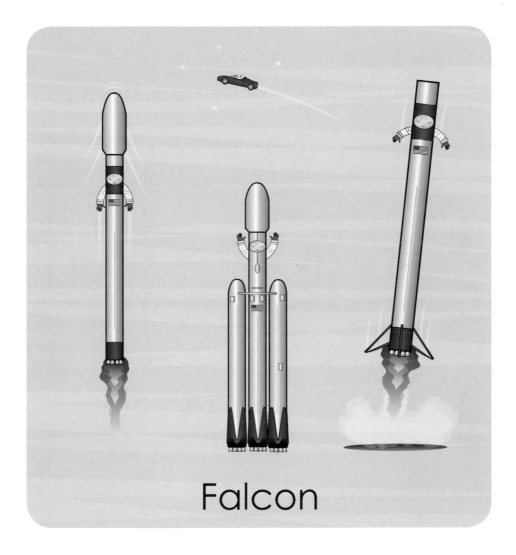

Falcon

Chapter 2
Moon Crew

This is one exclusive crew. There are not many things that have had the privilege of journeying to our lovely shiny Moon. To this day, just 12 men have walked on its dusty surface, and only a few tens of machines have made the 238,855-mi. (384,400km) journey. The United States's Apollo 11 was the first mission to land on the Moon, getting Neil Armstrong and Buzz Aldrin there and back in July 1969. Later Apollo missions carried the Moonbuggy—a vehicle that bumped and bounced across the Moon. Now, it's China's turn with its Chang'e robotic missions blasting off to visit our old friend.

The Moon

Apollo 11

Moonbuggy

Chang'e

The Moon
■ Moon Crew

☀ The brightest thing in the night sky but has no light of its own
☀ The Moon is drifting away from Earth by 1.2 in. (3cm) each year
☀ It took Apollo 11 three days to journey to the Moon

I am Earth's faithful friend. Slowly spinning around the planet, I'm a chip off the old block. I formed about 4,500 million years ago, when a Mars-sized asteroid smashed into Earth. I turn gracefully as I orbit so, like dancers, the same side of me always faces Earth. This means that I have a "far side" that you never see unless you visit me.

The story of the Moon landings began in 1961 with a promise from U.S. President JFK that the U.S.A. would send a man to visit (and return him safely) "before this decade is out." Neil Armstrong landed on my surface in 1969 and, in 1972, the last astronaut on the Moon, Eugene Cernan, left his footprints and daughter's initials in the lunar dust. With no air and no wind, the footprints of the astronauts who walked across me will stay there forever.

- Diameter: 2,159 mi. (3,475km)
- Average distance from Earth: 238,855 mi. (384,400km)
- Time taken to orbit Earth: 27.3 days
- Number of astronauts to visit Moon: 12
- Total time spent on Moon: 154 hours, 18 minutes

The Moon

Apollo 11
Moon Crew

✴ Three-stage lunar mission, launched by Saturn V rocket
✴ The lunar module landed on the Moon on July 20, 1969
✴ This tin can was nicknamed "Eagle"

I am an all-American hero. Six hundred million people worldwide tuned in to watch me take the first astronauts to the Moon, live on TV. Neil Armstrong took the "Eagle" down to the surface with Buzz Aldrin, missing the landing spot by 4 mi. (6.4km). Meanwhile Michael Collins stayed in orbit in my Command Module (CM). Stepping out onto the Moon, Armstrong uttered the immortal words, "That's one small step for [a] man, one giant leap for mankind."

It took nearly 400,000 engineers and scientists to get me into space. They built the largest rocket ever seen—the giant Saturn V. The two astronauts stayed on the Moon for almost a day, collecting samples, setting up experiments, and taking photographs. Then the Eagle blasted off once more to meet up with the CM and coast back to Earth.

● Height of Saturn V rocket: 364 ft. (111m)
● Mass of Saturn V: 3,200 tons (2,900,000kg) (650 elephants)
● Time "Eagle" spent on the surface of the Moon: 21.5 hours

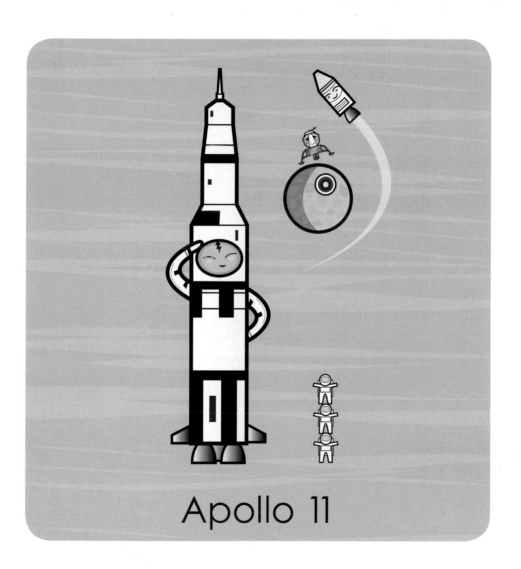

Apollo 11

Moonbuggy
■ Moon Crew

✳ The last word in electric-powered off-road vehicles
✳ This nippy cart was used on Apollo missions 15, 16, and 17
✳ Its official name is Lunar Roving Vehicle (LRV)

What's better than walking on the Moon? Why, surely, it's driving on the Moon! With my light, aluminum frame, mesh wheels, and nylon-strapping bucket seats, I allowed astronauts to range much farther than they had on previous landings. I was transported to the Moon on the last three Apollo missions, strapped to the outside of the lunar module, just like dirt bikes on an RV!

Moonbuggy

● Longest single trip: 12.5 mi. (20.1km)
● Lunar land-speed record: 11 mph (18km/h) (Eugene Cernan)
● Power: 2 x 36-V batteries

Chang'e
Moon Crew

* ☀ Chinese missions named after the Chinese Moon goddess
* ☀ Only U.S.A, Russia, and China have landed on the Moon so far
* ☀ China aims to put a human on the Moon by 2036

Chang'e

I am a family of Chinese lunar spacecraft sent to explore our beautiful companion. Chang'e 1 and 2 were orbiters. Chang'e 3, which visited in 2013, had a rover as well as the lander (still going strong four years later). Chang'e 4, launched in 2018, will make China the first country to land space hardware on the far side of the Moon. Pass the mooncakes!

* ● Name of Chang'e 3 rover: Yutu ("Jade Rabbit")
* ● No. of wheels: 6
* ● Mass: 310 lb. (140kg)

Chapter 3
Sunshine Superstars

These Sun-skimming superheroes are the spacecraft tasked with exploring our star and the rocky terrestrial planets orbiting close to it—Mercury, Venus, Earth, and Mars. These guys withstand SIZZLING temperatures—hot enough to make exposed metal reach 500°F (260°C)— and a barrage of circuit-frying radiation from the Sun. Many of them turn their instruments back on Earth, to study our home planet in ever-greater detail. Mighty Mars is a popular destination, but so many have been lost on these missions that astro-scientists joke about a "Great Galactic Ghoul" who feeds on Mars probes. Shudder!

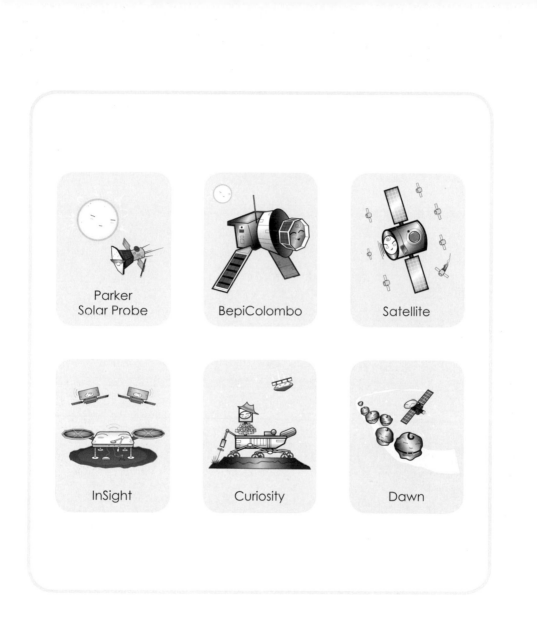

Parker
Solar Probe

BepiColombo

Satellite

InSight

Curiosity

Dawn

Parker Solar Probe
Sunshine Superstars

☀ Will get closer to the Sun than any human-made object
☀ This car-size probe will dip into the Sun's outer atmosphere
☀ Science will help us understand the Sun and other stars

A solar explorer, and the closest a spacecraft has ever got to our home star, I am on a mission to touch the Sun. Having left Earth in summer 2018, I'm going to swoop to within four million miles (six million km) of the Sun's surface, flying into the teeth of howling solar wind and blazing radiation as I dive in and out of the Sun's atmosphere. Temperatures will hit a sizzling 2,498°F (1,370°C)—let's hope my heat shield does its job!

Neither brave nor foolish, I'm built for the job of exploring the solar wind. This stream of electrified hot gas blasts from the Sun's surface and into space. By getting close to it, I aim to answer some long-standing questions about how stars work. I will also help scientists understand and forecast space weather to better protect astronauts and satellites in orbit around the planet.

● PSP speed: 125 mi. per second (200km per second) (430,000 mph/700,000kph)
● Heat shield thickness: 4.5 in. (11.4cm)
● Heat shield mass: 160 lb. (72.5kg)

Parker Solar Probe

BepiColombo
Sunshine Superstars

✳ BepiColombo spaceship to Mercury is made of three parts
✳ Joint mission between European and Japanese space agencies
✳ Named after Italian scientist, Giuseppe "Bepi" Colombo

I'm one talented piece of space tech—two parts scientific instrument and one part power unit. My Mercury Transfer Module (MTM) has the boosters and juice for the long cruise to the "hot potato" planet.

To slot into orbit, I'll have to time my braking perfectly! I have four xenon thrusters to make sure I get it right. Once there, my twin explorers—the Mercury Planetary Orbiter (MPO) and the Mercury Magnetospheric Orbiter (MMO)—will measure the planet's surface and interior, and its magnetic field. They'll be working in hardcore conditions. On Mercury's sunlit face, temperatures soar to about 800°F (400°C)—the same as a pizza oven—while on the night side, they plummet to a chilly –310°F (–190°C). Then, there's the Sun's intense radiation . . . it's a blast!

● Launch date: October 2018
● Number of planetary flybys: Earth (1); Venus (2); Mercury (6)
● Arrival at Mercury: December 2025

BepiColombo

Satellite
Sunshine Superstars

* An automatic, computer-controlled machine, orbiting Earth
* Has power, thrusters, control systems, an antenna, and radio
* Satellites in the night sky look like little, steadily moving stars

Swinging silently overhead, I watch the planet and keep people in touch with each other. I'm built in "clean rooms," where air is filtered and engineers wear special gear. One speck of dust on my sensitive equipment can ruin a multi-million-dollar mission. Please don't sneeze!

I am launched from near the equator, because Earth spins faster around its middle so it takes less energy to get me into space. Earth observation, or "remote-sensing," satellites monitor changes on the planet's surface, map the ocean floor, and track the weather. Communications satellites carry TV, radio, and your phone calls. Global Positioning Systems (GPS) quickly calculate your position so you never get lost. Sometimes I spy on people, too. I mostly spin in "low Earth orbit" (LEO) close to the planet.

- First communications satellite: Telstar (1962)
- Low Earth Orbit: 75 to 1,240 mi. (120 to 2,000km) above Earth
- Geostationary orbit: approx 22,350 mi. (36,000km) above Earth

Satellite

InSight
Sunshine Superstars

✳ The first lander to peer inside the Red Planet
✳ Briefcase-sized mini satellites send its data back to Earth
✳ Seeks to learn more about the formation of the rocky planets

I'm a Mars medic, a planetary practitioner. Pack my battered briefcase, I'm paying a house visit to the Red Planet. They call me "InSight" because my full name isn't very catchy. I am the Interior Exploration using Seismic Investigations, Geodesy, and Heat Transport.

In my two years on Mars, I'll investigate the planet's rocky insides. I'll check its pulse, listening in on the way sounds from "marsquakes" and meteor impacts travel through its interior. I'll take its temperature, measuring the heat flow inside it. And I'll measure its "core reflexes"—how the core wobbles as it travels around the Sun. By comparing my data with the same information about Earth, we will learn more about how rocky planets formed, helping us to know something about rocky planets orbiting distant stars.

● Launch date: May 2018
● Arrival on Mars: November 2018
● Landing site: Elysium Planitia, Mars

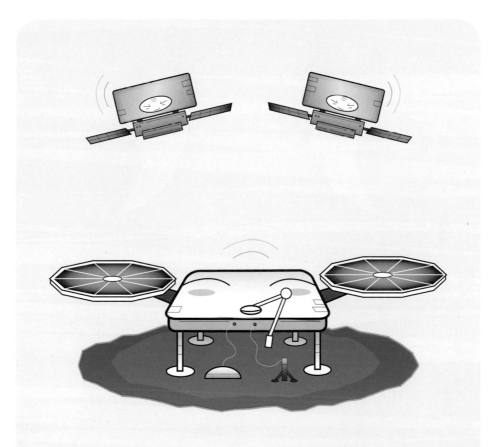

InSight

Curiosity
Sunshine Superstars

✳ NASA's Mars Science Laboratory (MSL) rover
✳ Curiosity is unmanned and controlled exclusively from Earth
✳ You can follow Curiosity's progress on Twitter

Call me Rover! I am a car-size puppy, super-keen and ready to explore—the ultimate remote-controlled robot. I'm sniffing around for the scent of life on the Red Planet.

I landed in Gale Crater in 2012 after the most incredible egg-drop in history. Nicknamed the "Seven Minutes of Terror," it involved an unlikely combination of parachute, "sky-crane," and rockets, but I touched down safely. I am a laboratory on wheels, with 17 high-tech cameras, a laser that can vaporize a rock at seven paces, a rock drill, and scientific instruments to analyze the chemical content of the Martian soil. Mars today is a dry, dead world, but if life once existed on the planet, it might have left chemical traces of its passing in the rocks. So far, no joy, but I'll keep on looking "doggedly"!

● Launch date: November 26, 2011
● Communications delay between Earth and Mars: about 14 minutes
● Top speed of travel: 295 ft. (90m) per hour (regular speed 98 ft./30m per hour)

Curiosity

Dawn
Sunshine Superstars

✴ NASA spacecraft visiting the asteroids Vesta and Ceres
✴ Tasked with learning about the formation of the solar system
✴ The first NASA probe to orbit two separate bodies

Mine was an ugly duckling mission that was canceled, reinstated, then postponed before finally getting off the ground. Once I took wing, however, I soared magnificently and exceeded everybody's expectations.

I roam the asteroid belt between Mars and Jupiter, to visit two of its largest members—both "starter planets" that stopped growing at an early age. I aim to find out how planets formed in the young solar system, and why it is that some hold on to water while others lose it. To get about, I use a propulsion engine called an ion drive. While Rocket works by throwing lots of mass behind it to generate thrust, my ion drive throws out very small masses at eye-watering speeds to achieve the same effect. It means I don't need to carry large amounts of heavy fuel with me. Zooooooom!

● Launch date: September 27, 2007
● Key dates: Vesta orbit entry: July 16, 2011; Ceres arrival: February 2015
● Length: 7.74 ft. (2.36m) (solar arrays retracted); 64.6 ft. (19.7m) (solar arrays extended)

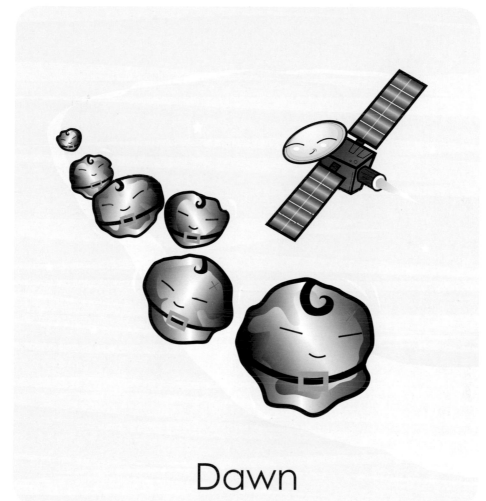

Dawn

Chapter 4
Outer-planetary Mob

Come and meet this hardened bunch of adventurers, the tough guys who mount expeditions to the outer planets, comets, and dwarf planets. Many of them belong to NASA's Flagship Program and count among the biggest and heaviest spacecraft ever launched. Short "launch windows" open when planets are reachable with a minimal outlay of energy. It means that space probes can minimize fuel and maximize onboard science equipment. Out in the wilds of the solar system, the cold and lack of sunlight make power a big issue. All of these explorers will perish out in space and none will ever return to Earth. . .

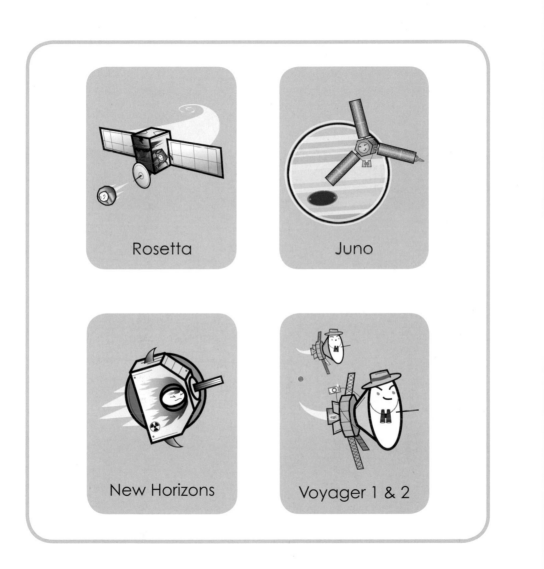

Rosetta

Juno

New Horizons

Voyager 1 & 2

Rosetta
■ Outer-planetary Mob

☀ A probe that made the first close-up investigation of a comet
☀ Rosetta sent lander Philae onto 67P/Churyumov-Gerasimenko
☀ Before Rosetta, a close study of comets lasted only a few hours

I'm an interstellar adventurer sent to unravel the mysteries of the solar system. I traveled for 10 years to discover how things were before the first planets formed. By catching up with comet 67P/Churyumov-Gerasimenko, I peered back 4,600 million years to a time when only comets and asteroids swirled around the Sun.

My twisted route took me whizzing past Earth and on a risky skim around the dark side of Mars, before voyaging to the "main belt" of asteroids. In 2014, I dispatched my lander, Philae, to the comet. The world watched as plucky Philae dived toward the icy surface . . . Sadly, the robot bounced and ended up in shadow, where its solar-powered batteries eventually died. After two fruitful years studying the comet, I crashed deliberately into it.

● Launch date: March 2, 2004
● Mass: 6,614 lb (3,000kg)
● Dimensions: 6.8 x 6.5 ft (2.8 x 2.1m)

Rosetta

Juno
■ Outer-planetary Mob

✺ Farseeing space probe that reached Jupiter in 2016
✺ On a mission to reveal the inner secrets of the largest planet
✺ Named after Jupiter's wife in mythology

I'm a total legend. In Roman mythology, when chief god Jupiter got up to mischief, he hid under clouds, but his wife, Juno, always saw right through them. I'm the same. This giant planet is made of gases that form coffee-and-cream colored bands of cloud, but they won't block me!

I'm tough, too—to reach my orbit here, I survived the most intense radiation a spacecraft has ever endured. I peer through Jupiter's clouds to measure the planet's gravity, magnetic fields, and winds. I have learned that Jupiter's gassy atmosphere goes a whopping 1,864 mi. (3,000km) below cloud level. I also snap pictures. My new views on this old planet include no less than eight massive cyclones at the north pole in 2017.

● Frequency of Jupiter orbits: once around the planet every fortnight
● Distance to Jupiter's cloud tops: 3,100 mi. (5,000km)
● Speed of Jupiter's surface winds: 225 mph (360km/h)

Juno

New Horizons

■ Outer-planetary Mob

☀ The spacecraft on a white-knuckle ride to Pluto and beyond
☀ Made a successful Jupiter flyby in late 2006
☀ The first spacecraft to make a flyby of Pluto

I'm a speed freak. Oh yeah, man! I set the record for the fastest launch from Earth, flung by an Atlas V rocket like a skimming stone across the blackness of space at 36,372 mi. (58,500km) per hour . . . a skipping stone the size of a grand piano!

I'm visiting distant parts of the solar system—where no other spacecraft have been before. When you travel this deep into space, far away from the Sun, solar panels are of no use. I have an onboard nuclear power plant to keep me going! My mission? To study the dwarf planet Pluto and its geology, climate, and five moons. I passed within 7,650 mi. (12,742km) of Pluto and 17,900 mi. (28,800km) of its largest moon, Charon. But why stop there? I have the unexplored, dark, and icy Kuiper Belt in my sights!

● Launch date: January 19, 2006
● Pluto encounter: July 14, 2015
● First images of Pluto released: November 28, 2006

New Horizons

Voyager 1 & 2
■ Outer-planetary Mob

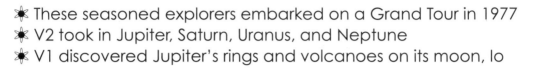

✳ These seasoned explorers embarked on a Grand Tour in 1977
✳ V2 took in Jupiter, Saturn, Uranus, and Neptune
✳ V1 discovered Jupiter's rings and volcanoes on its moon, Io

Veterans from another era, we are the longest-serving spacecraft. We have looped through the solar system and are traveling into interstellar space. Currently over 145 times more distant from Earth than the Sun is, we are officially the most remote human-made objects.

We have visited the four biggest planets, sending home incredible snapshots. In 1990, Voyager 1 looked back at Earth and took a famous series of shots showing our planet as a "pale blue dot," half a pixel big. Voyager 1's last action will be to study the "magnetic highway" at the edge of the Sun's influence. Sadly, our electrical supply will begin to run low in about 2020, and although our controllers will shut down our systems one-by-one to prolong our lives, we oldies will finally blink out in 2025.

● Launch dates: August 20, 1977 (V2); September 5, 1977 (V1)
● Distance from Earth: 13.2 billion mi. (21.3 billion km) (V1, July 2018)
● Number of work years devoted to the Voyager project: 11,000

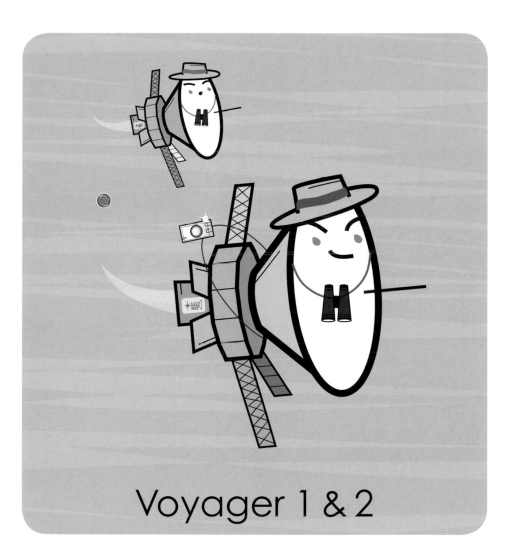

Voyager 1 & 2

Chapter 5
Infinity and Beyond

With their sharp eyes firmly fixed on the glories of the universe and their dials set to "infinity and beyond," these go-getters seek the bigger picture. These critters are the über-geeks of space exploration—the ones who ask the most important questions about our 13.7-billion-year-old cosmos. Questions like: How did it all begin? (Planck); What does it look like? (Gaia); What is it made of? (Space Telescope); and is there anyone else out there . . . anyone at all? (TESS). Hitch a ride with these high-tech dudes and it won't be long before you start hearing some answers. Prepare to be mind-boggled!

Space
Telescope

Planck

TESS

Gaia

Space Telescope
Infinity and Beyond

☀ Star of NASA's Great Observatories Program
☀ This eye-above-the-sky shows the universe in close-up
☀ The James Webb Space Telescope is set to launch in 2021

I'm a real paparazzo—I take photos of *actual* stars! Orbiting Earth, I have great views of objects in the solar system, but I spend most of my time peering into the Milky Way and beyond, into the great depths of space and time.

Of course there are powerful telescopes on Earth, too, but they mainly collect "visible light" images—ones that can be seen with the human eye. I, on the other hand, can tinker with X-ray and infrared images, which puts me in a different league altogether. I've shown observers what far-distant objects, such as galaxies, look like in close-up. Better still, I have revealed the very first galaxies created at the beginning of time. I've also shed light on the existence of extrasolar planets, and might have found the youngest star ever seen. Far out!

- Hubble Space Telescope (HST): provides "visible light" images of the universe
- Spitzer Space Telescope (SST): provides "infrared light" images of the universe
- Chandra X-ray Observatory (CXO): provides X-ray images of the universe

Space Telescope

Planck
■ Infinity and Beyond

※ An ESA mission sent to study the energy left by the big bang
※ It is checking the universe for signs of sudden "growth spurts"
※ Gives a supersharp, all-sky survey at microwave wavelengths

First things first: I'm no plank! My funny name comes from the famous German physicist, Max Planck. I'm an ambitious little 'scope with the enitre universe in my sights.

I want to find out what the universe was like way back when and the rate at which it's expanding. I'm measuring the soft glow of heat still remaining from the superhot explosion that kick-started the universe. These embers of the big bang are called the Cosmic Microwave Background (CMB). It's all around us, in every direction. The mystery I want to solve is how such a big, messy blast resulted in the "lumpy" universe we live in. You might expect an explosion to spread energy—and mass—evenly across space, but barely noticeable ripples gave rise to the galaxies of today's universe. I want to know why!

● Launch date: May 14, 2009
● Distance from Earth: 932,000 mi. (1.5 million km)
● Average temperature of CMB: –454°F (–270°C)

Planck

TESS
▪ Infinity and Beyond

※ Swivel-eyed space telescope that scans the entire sky
※ On a two-year mission to find targets for big telescopes
※ Aims to find 500 roughly Earth-sized planets

I'm TESS the planet hunter. Wheeling around Earth, my job is to scout for exoplanets—worlds outside our solar system that orbit other stars. My given name is Transiting Exoplanet Survey Satellite. I peer at distant stars to spot a planet as it crosses in front of—or "transits"—a star. I can't see the planet but I measure how much light it blocks out.

I'm on the lookout for habitable worlds. If the conditions are right on these planets, we might find living things there. Apart from what lives on Earth, we know of no other life in the universe. I swing from point to point, spending an entire month fixed on just one region in the sky, before moving to the next. I mostly focus on stars that are smaller and dimmer than our Sun. Anything I find, I mark for future studies.

● Number of stars to survey: more than 500,000
● Number of cameras: 4
● Time taken to orbit Earth: 13.7 days

TESS

Gaia
■ Infinity and Beyond

✴ Mission to make accurate 3-D maps of the Milky Way
✴ Measures the distances to stars and tracks their motion
✴ Also follows the position of more than 14,000 asteroids

I am the Mapmaker. Zipping through space, I've gotta plot the position, brightness, and color of more than a billion stars in our galaxy. That's just 1 percent of the stars in the Milky Way! I work at a breathtaking pace, measuring about 100,000 stars each minute.

In 2018, I released the most accurate space map of the galaxy . . . ever! As well as a staggering 1.7 billion stars mapped to high precision, I measured the movements of seven million stars and the surface temperatures of about 100 million. I checked each measurement 70 times to make sure it was correct. My map will help figure out the dance of the stars and the forces exerted on our galactic home. Once scientists explore my data, loads of major discoveries are bound to come tumbling out.

● Launch date: October 2013
● Orbital period: approximately 180 days
● Distance from Earth: 932,000 mi. (1.5 million km)

Gaia

Index

Pages that show characters are in **bold**

Glossary

Asteroid A small rock in orbit around the Sun between the orbits of Mars and Jupiter.

Atmosphere The layer of air that surrounds a star or planet. Beyond the atmosphere is space.

Big Bang The idea that the universe was created in an enormous, hot fireball about 13.7 billion years ago.

Comet A dirty snowball looping the Sun with a long, elliptical (oval) orbit. Comets have one or two tails and, unlike planets, can appear in any part of the sky.

Constellation An area of the sky containing a pattern made by stars, as seen from Earth. Stars in the same constellation are at different distances from Earth.

Cyclone A spinning storm that travels around an area of low atmospheric pressure.

Extrasolar planet A planet orbiting a different star than the Sun; belongs to an entirely different planetary system.

Galaxy A system of billions of stars, dust, and gas clouds (and sometimes black holes) held together by gravitational attraction.

Gravity The invisible force of attraction felt between objects that have mass. Gravity keeps the planets orbiting the Sun and the Moon orbiting Earth.

Interstellar space The regions of space in between the stars, and beyond the influence of a star's "weather."

Infrared Frequencies of electromagnetic radiation just

below visible light. It is invisible to the human eye.

Invisible universe Objects in space that "shine" in those parts of the electromagnetic spectrum that are above and below the frequency of visible light.

Kevlar A very strong artificial fiber used in space suits to protect astronauts from space hazards.

Launch window The period of time when Earth's spin and its position on its orbit enable a spacecraft to be launched on its journey.

Magnetic field The invisible area of magnetism that surrounds a magnet.

Mass A measure of the amount of matter in an object. Things with mass feel weight when attracted to another object by the force of gravity.

Microwave Short-wavelength, high-frequency radio waves are known as microwaves.

Milky Way Our home galaxy—a barred spiral galaxy. Our solar system is located on the inner rim of one of its arms.

Orbital period The time taken for an object to make one complete revolution (orbit) around another body.

Payload Equipment carried by a rocket or launch vehicle. Payloads are stored in the payload bay.

Radiation Energy emitted by a body in the form of electromagnetic radiation (e.g. light) or fast-moving particles, smaller than an atom.

Glossary

Satellite An object that orbits a planet. The Moon is a natural satellite. Artificial satellites gather and send information back to Earth.

Solar array A sheet of solar panels used to convert sunlight into electricity.

Solar system The family of planets, moons, asteroids, meteoroids, comets, dust, and debris that orbits the Sun.

Space Race A competition between nations to be the first to do something in space. The United States and U.S.S.R. raced against each other to put a man on the Moon in the 1950s and 1960s.

Static A crackling hiss that can be picked up by radios, TVs, phones, satellites, and radio telescopes. Most of it is generated by natural electricity on Earth—e.g. lightning—but a small portion comes from the big bang explosion.

Terrestrial planet A rocky planet, such as the four inner planets of the solar system.

Vacuum A region of space that contains almost no matter.

Velocity The speed of an object traveling in a particular direction.

Visible light The part of the electromagnetic spectrum to which a human's eyes are sensitive.

X-ray High frequency electromagnetic radiation. We can't see X-rays because their frequency is higher than visible light.